DONNER PARTY MEMORIAL, SALT LAKE CITY, UTAH

ACROSS THE PLAINS IN THE DONNER PARTY
a personal narrative of the overland trip to California
1846-47
by Virginia Reed Murphy

Library of Congress Cataloging-in-Publication Data

Murphy, Virginia Reed, b. 1834?
    Across the Plains in the Donner Party : a personal narrative of
the overland trip to California, 1846-47 / by Virginia Reed Murphy :
with illustrations by Frederic Remington and others.
      p.   cm.
  Previously published: Golden, Colo. : Outbooks, 1980.
  ISBN 0-89646-063-0
  1. Donner Party. 2. Overland journeys to the Pacific. 3. Murphy,
Virginia Reed. b. 1834?--Journeys. I. Title.
F868.N5M8 1995
979.4'03'092--dc20
                                     95-40419
                                        CIP

a publishing and
distributing company

Since 1972

VISTABOOKS
Box 29D/Blue River Rt
Silverthorne, CO 80498

ISBN 0-89646-063-0

Emigrants Crossing the Plains.

4

Emigrant Trail across Skull Valley

OLD TRAIL CROSSING HORSESHOE CREEK, A TRIBUTARY OF THE PLATTE.

ACROSS THE PLAINS IN THE DONNER PARTY:
a personal narrative of the overland trip to California
1846-47
by Virginia Reed Murphy

EDITOR'S PREFACE

Our author, then Virginia Reed, age 12, left Springfield, Illinois, the bright spring morning of April 14, 1846, with her family plus 25 fellow emigrants, their wagons, oxen, horses, and all worldly possessions.

On May 29th, in Kansas, her grandmother died and was buried on the trail.

In July in Wyoming her pony could not keep up and was left.

In September in Utah her family lost its oxen and had to abandon a wagon with their possessions.

In October, in Nevada, her stepfather killed a man and was banished from the train.

In November, her party tried to cross the Sierra Nevada of California, but the snow was already too deep and they made camp on the shore of Donner Lake to await their fate. As a result, 13 of those who started with her from Springfield, and 29 more who joined her along the way, never did cross those mountains.

This is her story, recalled 45 years after the tragic event, when she was a woman of 56 and a mother of six children, residing in San Jose, California. It was written at the request of Robert Underwood Johnson, then an editor for the national magazine *Century*, and published in 1891 as part of a series of first-person articles done by those who had made Western American history. (Other topics included Custer's last battle, the California gold rush, and John Muir's pleas for Yosemite.)

VIRGINIA E. REED.
(Mrs. J. M. Murphy.)
1880.

Virginia was an excellent choice for the chronicler of the party: at the time of the trip she was old enough to correctly observe events and impressionable enough to remember them yet not prejudiced due to being involved in the decisions. Her stepfather, James Reed, was perhaps more the Donner Party leader than the chosen one, George Donner. Donner had had difficulty in that role throughut the trip, and then suffered an injury that led to illness and death. Even though banished from the train, Reed played a further pivotal role for the group in that he went on to California, pled for help, organized relief parties, and then himself crossed back to the mountain camps. Probably with some significance, he and his entire family survived.

The Donner Party's story immediately became a part of the American epic, and it remains so today. Monuments and historic parks dot the route of their trek across the U.S., for they symbolized in extreme the hardships all emigrants faced—and the chances they took. Most winters, for instance, Donner Pass can be crossed in November, though not in the unlucky November of 1846.

Why did they try to emigrate across the U.S.? They were bound for California and the rich agricultural lands reported to be there, of course. And theirs was an early attempt. The Mormons had not yet arrived at Salt Lake City, and the gold discovery that was to inspire the rush of 1849 had not yet been made. Nevertheless, there was a trail for part of the way, and even an emigrants' handbook. John Fremont had made a map of sorts to use, and there were other travelers en route to share information with—not always reliably it turned out. The trip was risky enough even when taken conservatively, and, unfortunately for little Virginia, the party she was with proved willing to gamble with the unknown.

We have reprinted the text exactly as written. Illustrations are from the original article with others added from contemporary sources, as *Century* for 1890, *History of the Donner Party* (1880), *Explorations in the Valley of the Great Salt Lake* (1853), *Picturesque California* (1888), *History of Nevada County* (1888), *Marvels of the New West* (1893), *Oregon and California in 1848* (1864), *Annals of San Francisco* (1854), *Picturesque America* (1872), *Narrative of the U.S. Exploring Expedition* (1844), *Report of the Exploring Expedition to the Rocky Mountains* (1845).

William R. Jones
Series Editor

THE EMIGRANT TRAIL THROUGH THE BAD LANDS, WYOMING.

ACKNOWLEDGEMENTS: Aside from author Virginia Reed Murphy and *The Century* magazine, which contributed the original text and the illustrations by Fredric Remington, gratitude is expressed to the following for their contributions: California Department of Parks and Recreation, Utah State Historical Society, Nevada Historical Society, Bancroft Library of the University of California, and Western History Room of the Denver Public Library. Gary Hurelle of the National Park Service drew the map in the center, and personnel at Donner Lake State Park (in California) and Fort Laramie National Historic Site (in Wyoming) reviewed the materials.

8

From *Narrative of the U.S. Exploring Expedition* by Charles Wilkes

This early map is an example of the type of route information available to the Donner Party and other emigrants of 1846 as they planned their treks westward. Fremont wandered through the region of what is now Nevada and Utah in 1844, almost lost.

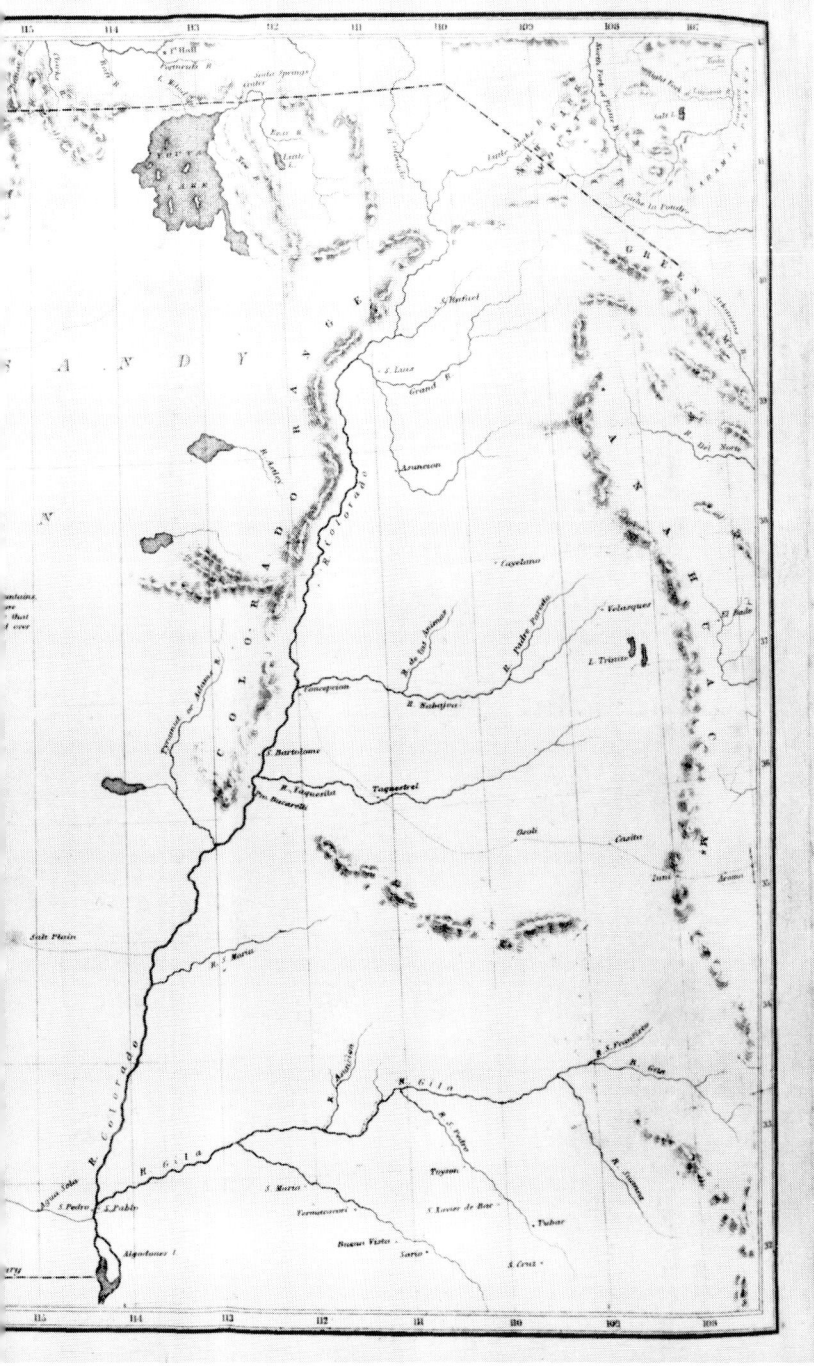

Later there would be good maps, marked routes, and detailed handbooks for the overland trip, especially after the Mormon emigration to Salt Lake City beginning in 1847 and the hordes of '49ers on their way to the gold fields of California.

THE AUTHOR'S PARENTS, JAMES FRAZIER REED AND MARGARET REED, WHO SURVIVED THE
DONNER PARTY TRAIL ALONG WITH ALL THEIR CHILDREN. HER FATHER WAS THE EFFECTIVE
LEADER OF THE PARTY AND, ALTHOUGH BANISHED FROM THE TRAIN FOR HAVING KILLED A
MAN IN SELF-DEFENSE, RETURNED TO RESCUE THOSE TRAPPED BY THE SNOW.

W. TABER.

"A PIONEER PALACE CAR."

ADAPTED FROM A SKETCH BY A. P. HILL.

ACROSS THE PLAINS IN THE DONNER PARTY:

a personal narrative of the Overland Trip to California, 1846-47

by Virginia Reed Murphy

I WAS a child when we started to California, yet I remember the journey well and I have cause to remember it, as our little band of emigrants who drove out of Springfield, Illinois, that spring morning of 1846 have since been known in history as the "Ill-fated Donner party" of "Martyr Pioneers." My father, James F. Reed, was the originator of the party, and the Donner brothers, George and Jacob, who lived just a little way out of Springfield, decided to join him.

All the previous winter we were preparing for the journey — and right here let me say that we suffered vastly more from fear of the Indians before starting than we did on the plains; at least this was my case. In the long winter evenings Grandma Keyes used to tell me Indian stories. She had an aunt who had been taken prisoner by the savages in the early settlement of Virginia and Kentucky and had remained a captive in their hands five years before she made her escape. I was fond of these stories and evening after evening would go into grandma's room, sitting with my back close against the wall so that no warrior could slip behind me with a tomahawk. I would coax her to tell me more about her aunt, and would sit listening to the recital of the fearful deeds of the savages, until it seemed to me that everything in the room, from the high old-fashioned bed-posts down even to the shovel and tongs in the chimney corner, was transformed into the dusky tribe in paint and feathers, all ready for the war dance. So when I was told that we were going to California and would have to pass through a region peopled by Indians, you can imagine how I felt.

Our wagons, or the "Reed wagons," as they were called, were all made to order and I can say without fear of contradiction that nothing like our family wagon ever started across the plains. It was what might be called a two-story wagon or "Pioneer palace car," attached to a regular immigrant train. My mother, though a young woman, was not strong and had been

CROSSING WATER TO ESCAPE A PRAIRIE FIRE.

in delicate health for many years, yet when sorrows and dangers came upon her she was the bravest of the brave. Grandma Keyes, who was seventy-five years of age, was an invalid, confined to her bed. Her sons in Springfield, Gersham and James W. Keyes, tried to dissuade her from the long and fatiguing journey, but in vain; she would not be parted from my mother, who was her only daughter. So the car in which she was to ride was planned to give comfort. The entrance was on the side, like that of an old-fashioned stage coach, and one stepped into a small room, as it were, in the centre of the wagon. At the right and left were spring seats with comfortable high backs, where one could sit and ride with as much ease as on the seats of a Concord coach. In this little room was placed a tiny sheet-iron stove, whose pipe, running through the top of the wagon, was prevented by a circle of tin from setting fire to the canvas cover. A board about a foot wide extended over the wheels on either side the full length of the wagon, thus forming the foundation for a large and roomy second story in which were placed our beds. Under the spring seats were compartments in which were stored many articles useful for the journey, such as a well filled work basket and a full assortment of medicines, with lint and bandages for dressing wounds. Our clothing was packed — not in Saratoga trunks — but in strong canvas bags plainly marked. Some of mama's young friends added a looking-glass, hung directly opposite the door, in order, as they said, that my mother might not forget to keep her good looks, and strange to say, when we had to leave this wagon, standing like a monument on the Salt Lake desert, the glass was still unbroken. I have often thought how pleased the Indians must have been when they found this mirror which gave them back the picture of their own dusky faces.

We had two wagons loaded with provisions. Everything in that line was bought that could be thought of. My father started with supplies enough to last us through the first winter in California, had we made the journey in the usual time of six months. Knowing that books were always scarce in a new country, we also took a good library of standard works. We even took a cooking stove which never had had a fire in it, and was destined never to have, as we cachéd it in the desert. Certainly no family ever started across the plains with more provisions or a better outfit for the journey ; and yet we reached California almost destitute and nearly out of clothing.

The family wagon was drawn by four yoke of oxen, large Durham steers at the wheel. The other wagons were drawn by three yoke each. We had saddle horses and cows, and last but not least my pony. He was a beauty and his name was Billy. I can scarcely remember when I was taught to sit a horse. I only know that when a child of seven I was the proud owner of a pony and used to go riding with papa. That was the chief pleasure to which I looked forward in crossing the plains,

AN EMIGRANT ENCAMPMENT.

ABANDONED.

ON THE WAY TO THE PLATTE.

to ride my pony every day. But a day came when I had no pony to ride, the poor little fellow gave out. He could not endure the hardships of ceaseless travel. When I was forced to part with him I cried until I was ill, and sat in the back of the wagon watching him become smaller and smaller as we drove on, until I could see him no more.

Never can I forget the morning when we bade farewell to kindred and friends. The Donners were there, having driven in the evening before with their families, so that we might get an early start. Grandma Keyes was carried out of the house and placed in the wagon on a large feather bed, propped up with pillows. Her sons implored her to remain and end her days with them, but she could not be separated from her only daughter. We were surrounded by loved ones, and there stood all my little schoolmates who had come to kiss me good-by. My father with tears in his eyes tried to smile as one friend after another grasped his hand in a last farewell. Mama was overcome with grief. At last we were all in the wagons, the drivers cracked their whips, the oxen moved slowly forward and the long journey had begun.

Could we have looked into the future and have seen the misery before us, these lines would never have been written. But we were full of hope and did not dream of sorrow. I can now see our little caravan of ten or twelve wagons as we drove out of old Springfield, my little black-eyed sister Patty sitting upon the bed, holding up the wagon cover so that Grandma might have a last look at her old home.

That was the 14th day of April, 1846. Our party numbered thirty-one, and consisted chiefly of three families, the other members being young men, some of whom came as drivers. The Donner family were George and Tamsen Donner and their five children, and Jacob and Elizabeth Donner and their seven children. Our family numbered nine, not counting three drivers — my father and mother, James Frazier and Margaret W. Reed, Grandma Keyes, my little sister Patty (now Mrs. Frank Lewis, of Capitola), and two little brothers, James F. Reed, Jr., and Thomas K. Reed, Eliza Williams and her brother Baylis, and lastly myself. Eliza had been a domestic in our family for many years, and was anxious to see California.

Many friends camped with us the first night out and my uncles traveled on for several days before bidding us a final farewell. It seemed strange to be riding in ox-teams, and we children were afraid of the oxen, thinking they

INITIALS OF THE AUTHOR'S FATHER, J. F. REED, CARVED IN ROCK AT ALCOVE SPRINGS, KANSAS, NEAR THE START OF THEIR FATEFUL TRIP.

could go wherever they pleased as they had no bridles. Milt Elliott, a knight of the whip, drove our family wagon. He had worked for years in my father's large saw-mill on the Sangamon River. The first bridge we came to, Milt had to stop the wagon and let us out. I remember that I called to him to be sure to make the oxen hit the bridge, and not to forget that grandma was in the wagon. How he laughed at the idea of the oxen missing the bridge! I soon found that Milt, with his "whoa," "haw," and "gee," could make the oxen do just as he pleased.

Nothing of much interest happened until we reached what is now Kansas. The first Indians we met were the Caws, who kept the ferry, and had to take us over the Caw River. I watched

A POWWOW WITH CHEYENNES.

them closely, hardly daring to draw my breath, and feeling sure they would sink the boat in the middle of the stream, and was very thankful when I found they were not like grandma's Indians. Every morning, when the wagons were ready to start, papa and I would jump on our horses, and go ahead to pick out a camping-ground. In our party were many who rode on horseback, but mama seldom did;

CROSSING OF THE PLATTE, MOUTH OF DEER CREEK

she preferred the wagon, and did not like to leave grandma, although Patty took upon herself this charge, and could hardly be persuaded to leave grandma's side. Our little home was so comfortable, that mama could sit reading and chatting with the little ones, and almost forget that she was really crossing the plains.

Grandma Keyes improved in health and spirits every day until we came to the Big Blue River, which was so swollen that we could not cross, but had to lie by and make rafts on which to take the wagons over. As soon as we stopped traveling, grandma began to fail, and on the 29th day of May she died. It seemed hard to bury her in the wilderness, and travel on, and we were afraid that the Indians would destroy her grave, but her death here, before our troubles began, was providential, and nowhere on the whole road could we have found so beautiful a resting place. By this time many emigrants had joined our company, and all turned out to assist at the funeral. A coffin was hewn out of a cottonwood tree, and John Denton, a young man from Springfield, found a large gray stone on which he carved with deep letters the name of "Sarah Keyes; born in Virginia," giving age and date of birth. She was buried under the shade of an oak, the slab being placed at the foot of the grave, on which were planted wild flowers growing in the sod. A minister in our party, the Rev. J. A. Cornwall, tried to give words of comfort as we stood about this lonely grave. Strange to say, that grave has never been disturbed; the wilderness blossomed into the city of Manhattan, Kansas, and we have been told that the city cemetery surrounds the grave of Sarah Keyes.

As the river remained high and there was no prospect of fording it, the men went to work cutting down trees, hollowing out logs and making rafts on which to take the wagons over. These logs, about twenty-five feet in length, were united by cross timbers, forming rafts, which were firmly lashed to stakes driven into the bank. Ropes were attached to both ends, by which the rafts were pulled back and forth across the river. The banks of this stream being steep, our heavily laden wagons had to be let down carefully with ropes, so that the wheels might run into the hollowed logs. This was no easy task when you take into consideration that in these wagons were women and children, who could cross the rapid river in no other way. Finally the dangerous work was accomplished and we resumed our journey.

The road at first was rough and led through a timbered country, but after striking the great valley of the Platte the road was good and the country beautiful. Stretching out before us as far as the eye could reach was a valley as green as emerald, dotted here and there with flowers of every imaginable color, and through this valley flowed the grand old Platte, a wide, rapid, shallow stream. Our company now numbered about forty wagons, and, for a time, we were commanded by Col. William H. Russell, then by George Donner. Exercise in the open air under bright skies, and freedom from peril combined to make this part of our journey an ideal pleasure trip. How I enjoyed riding my pony, galloping over the plain, gathering wild flowers! At night the young folks would gather about the camp fire chatting merrily, and often a song would be heard, or some clever dancer would give us a barn-door jig on the hind gate of a wagon.

Traveling up the smooth valley of the Platte, we passed Court House Rock, Chimney Rock and Scott's Bluffs, and made from fifteen to twenty miles a day, shortening or lengthening the distance in order to secure a good camping ground. At night when we drove into camp, our wagons were placed so as to form a circle or corral, into which our cattle were driven, after grazing, to prevent the Indians from stealing them, the camp-fires and tents being on the outside. There were many expert riflemen in the party and we never lacked for game. The plains were alive with buffalo, and herds could be seen every day coming to the Platte to drink. The meat of the young buffalo is excellent and so is that of the antelope, but the antelope are so fleet of foot it is difficult to get a shot at one. I witnessed many a buffalo hunt and more than once was in the chase close beside my father. A buffalo will not attack one unless wounded. When he sees the hunter he raises his shaggy head, gazes at him for a moment, then turns and runs; but when he is wounded he will face his pursuer. The only danger lay in a stampede, for nothing could withstand the onward rush of these massive creatures, whose tread seemed to shake the prairie.

Antelope and buffalo steaks were the main article on our bill-of-fare for weeks, and no tonic was needed to give zest for the food; our appetites were a marvel. Eliza soon discovered that cooking over a camp fire was far different from cooking on a stove or range, but all hands assisted her. I remember that she had the cream all ready for the churn as we drove into the South Fork of the Platte, and while we were fording the grand old stream she went on with her work, and made several pounds of butter. We found no trouble in

A HERD OF BUFFALOES AT THE PLATTE.

18

crossing the Platte, the only danger being in quicksand. The stream being wide, we had to stop the wagon now and then to give the oxen a few moments' rest. At Fort Laramie, two hundred miles farther on, we celebrated the fourth of July in fine style. Camp was pitched earlier than usual and we prepared a grand dinner. Some of my father's friends in Springfield had given him a bottle of good old brandy, which he agreed to drink at a certain hour of this day looking to the east, while his friends in Illinois were to drink a toast to his success from a companion bottle with their faces turned west, the difference in time being carefully estimated; and at the hour agreed upon, the health of our friends in Springfield was drunk with great enthusiasm. At Fort Laramie was a party of Sioux, who were on the war path going to fight the Crows or Blackfeet. The Sioux are fine-looking Indians and I was not in the least afraid of them. They fell in love with my pony and set about bargaining to buy him. They brought buffalo robes and beautifully tanned buckskin, pretty beaded moccasins, and ropes made of grass, and placing these articles in a heap alongside several of their ponies, they made my father understand by signs that they would give them all for Billy and his rider. Papa smiled and shook his head; then the number of ponies was increased and, as a last tempting inducement, they brought an old coat, that

CHIMNEY ROCK, ON THE NORTH PLATTE,

had been worn by some poor soldier, thinking my father could not withstand the brass buttons!

On the sixth of July we were again on the march. The Sioux were several days in passing our caravan, not on account of the length of our train, but because there were so many Sioux. Owing to the fact that our wagons

SCOTT'S BLUFFS

FORT LARAMIE IN 1849.

were strung so far apart, they could have massacred our whole party without much loss to themselves. Some of our company became alarmed, and the rifles were cleaned out and loaded, to let the warriors see that we were prepared to fight; but the Sioux never showed any inclination to disturb us. Their curiosity was annoying, however, and our wagon with its conspicuous stove-pipe and looking-glass attracted their attention. They were continually swarming about trying to get a look at themselves in the mirror, and their desire to possess my pony was so strong that at last I had to ride in the wagon and let one of the drivers take charge of Billy. This I did not like, and in order to see how far back the line of warriors extended, I picked up a large field-glass which hung on a rack, and as I pulled it out with a click, the warriors jumped back, wheeled their ponies and scattered. This pleased me greatly, and I told my mother I could fight the whole Sioux tribe with a spyglass, and as revenge for forcing me to ride in the wagon, whenever they came near trying to get a peep at their war-paint and feathers, I would raise the glass and laugh to see them dart away in terror.

A new route had just been opened by Lansford W. Hastings, called the "Hastings Cutoff," which passed along the southern shore of the Great Salt Lake rejoining the old "Fort Hall Emigrant" road on the Humboldt. It was said to shorten the distance three hundred miles. Much time was lost in debating which course to pursue; Bridger and Vasques, who were in charge of the fort, sounded the praises of the new road. My father was so eager to reach California that he was quick to take advantage of any means to shorten the distance, and we were assured by Hastings and his party that the only bad part was the forty-mile drive through the desert by the shore of the lake.

O'FALLON'S BLUFFS FROM NEAR THE JUNCTION OF THE FORKS OF THE PLATTE.

FORT BRIDGER. BLACK'S FORK OF GREEN RIVER.

None of our party knew then, as we learned afterwards, that these men had an interest in the road, being employed by Hastings. But for the advice of these parties we should have continued on the old Fort Hall road. Our company had increased in numbers all along the line, and was now composed of some of the very best people and some of the worst. The greater portion of our company went by the old road and reached California in safety. Eighty-seven persons took the "Hastings Cut-off," including the Donners, Breens, Reeds, Murphys (not the Murphys of Santa Clara County), C. T. Stanton, John Denton, Wm. McClutchen, Wm. Eddy, Louis Keseburg, and many others too numerous to mention in a short article like this. And these are the unfortunates who have since been known as the "Donner Party."

On the morning of July 31 we parted with our traveling companions, some of whom had become very dear friends, and, without a suspicion of impending disaster, set off in high spirits on the "Hastings Cut-off"; but a few days showed us that the road was not as it had been represented. We were seven days in reaching Weber Cañon, and Hastings, who was guiding a party in advance of our train, left a note by the wayside warning us that the road through Weber Cañon was impassable and advising us to select a road over the mountains, the outline of which he attempted to give on paper. These directions were so vague that C. T. Stanton, William Pike, and my father

A PERIL OF THE PLAINS.

rode on in advance and overtook Hastings and tried to induce him to return and guide our party. He refused, but came back over a portion of the road, and from a high mountain endeavored to point out the general course. Over this road my father traveled alone, taking notes, and blazing trees, to assist him in retracing his course, and reaching camp after an absence of four days. Learning of the hardships of the advance train, the party decided

A BIT OF ROUGH ROAD.

to cross towards the lake. Only those who have passed through this country on horseback can appreciate the situation. There was absolutely no road, not even a trail. The cañon wound around among the hills. Heavy underbrush had to be cut away and used for making a road bed. While cutting our way step by step through the "Hastings Cut-off," we were overtaken and joined by the Graves family, consisting of W. F. Graves, his wife and eight children, his son-in-law Jay Fosdick, and a young man by the name of John Snyder. Finally we reached the end of the cañon where it looked as though our wagons would have to be abandoned. It seemed impossible for the oxen to pull them up the steep hill and the bluffs beyond, but we doubled teams and the work was, at last, accomplished, almost every yoke in the train being required to pull up each wagon. While in this cañon Stanton and Pike came into camp; they had suffered greatly on account of the exhaustion of their horses and had come near perishing. Worn with travel and greatly discouraged we reached the shore of the Great Salt Lake. It had taken an entire month, instead of a week, and our cattle were not fit to cross the desert.

We were now encamped in a valley called "Twenty

NATURAL BRIDGE
ON LA PRÊLE RIVER.

22

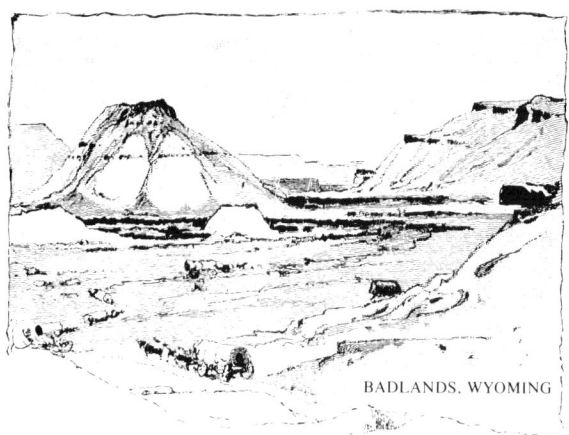

BADLANDS, WYOMING

Wells."* The water in these wells was pure and cold, welcome enough after the alkaline pools from which we had been forced to drink. We prepared for the long drive across the desert and laid in, as we supposed, an ample supply of water and grass. This desert had been represented to us as only forty miles wide but we found it nearer eighty. It was a dreary, desolate, alkali waste; not a living thing could be seen; it seemed as though the hand of death had been laid upon the country. We started in the evening, traveled all that night, and the following day and night — two nights and one day of suffering from thirst and heat by day and piercing cold by night. When the third night fell and we saw the barren waste stretching away apparently as boundless as when we started, my father determined to go ahead in search of water. Before starting he instructed the drivers, if the cattle showed signs of giving out to take them from the wagons and follow him. He had not been gone long before the oxen began to fall to the ground from thirst and exhaustion. They were unhitched at once and driven ahead. My father coming back met the drivers with the cattle within ten miles of water and instructed them to return as soon as the animals had satisfied their thirst. He reached us about daylight. We waited all that day in the desert looking for the return of our drivers, the other wagons going on out of sight. Towards night the situation became desperate and we had only a few drops of water left; another night there meant death. We must set out on foot and try to reach some of the wagons. Can I ever forget that night in the desert, when we walked mile after mile in the darkness, every step seeming to be the very last

*Now Grantsville, Utah.

FIRST VIEW OF GREAT SALT LAKE
This summit is probably ''Big Mountain,'' crossed by the Donner Party on August 20, 1846.

Salt Lake.

GREAT DESERT TO THE WEST OF SALT LAKE.

we could take! Suddenly all fatigue was banished by fear; through the night came a swift rushing sound of one of the young steers crazed by thirst and apparently bent upon our destruction. My father, holding his youngest child in his arms and keeping us all close behind him, drew his pistol, but finally the maddened beast turned and dashed off into the darkness. Dragging ourselves along about ten miles, we reached the wagon of Jacob Donner. The family were all asleep, so we children lay down on the ground. A bitter wind swept over the desert, chilling us through and through. We crept closer together, and, when we complained of the cold, papa placed all five of our dogs around us, and only for the warmth of these faithful creatures we should doubtless have perished.

At daylight papa was off to learn the fate of his cattle, and was told that all were lost, except one cow and an ox. The stock, scenting the water, had rushed on ahead of the men, and had probably been stolen by the Indians, and driven into the mountains, where all traces of them were lost. A week was spent here on the edge of the desert in a fruitless search. Almost every man in the company turned out, hunting in all directions, but our eighteen head of cattle were never found. We had lost our best yoke of oxen before reaching Bridger's Fort from drinking poisoned water found standing in pools, and had bought at the fort two yoke of young steers, but now all were gone, and my father and his family were left in the desert, eight hundred

A DESPERATE SITUATION.

WATER!

miles from California, seemingly helpless. We realized that our wagons must be abandoned. The company kindly let us have two yoke of oxen, so with our ox and cow yoked together we could bring one wagon, but, alas! not the one which seemed so much like a home to us, and in which grandma had died. Some of the company went back with papa and assisted him in cacheing everything that could not be packed in one wagon. A cache was made by digging a hole in the ground, in which a box or the bed of a wagon was placed. Articles to be buried were packed into this box, covered with boards, and the earth thrown in upon them, and thus they were hidden from sight. Our provisions were divided among the company. Before leaving the desert camp, an inventory of provisions on hand was taken, and it was found that the supply was not sufficient to last us through to California, and as if to render the situation more terrible, a storm came on during the night and the hill-tops became white with snow. Some one must go on to Sutter's Fort after provisions. A call was made for volunteers. C. T. Stanton and Wm. McClutchen bravely offered their services and started on bearing letters from the company to Captain Sutter asking for relief. We resumed our journey

PALISADE CAÑON.

by Thomas Moran

and soon reached Gravelly Ford on the Humboldt.

I now come to that part of my narrative which delicacy of feeling for both the dead and the living would induce me to pass over in silence, but which a correct and lucid chronicle of subsequent events of historical impor-

tance will not suffer to be omitted. On the 5th day of October, 1846, at Gravelly Ford, a tragedy was enacted which affected the subsequent lives and fortunes of more than one member of our company. At this point in our journey we were compelled to double our teams in order to ascend a steep, sandy hill. Milton Elliott, who was driving our wagon, and John Snyder, who was driving one of Mr. Graves's, became involved in a quarrel over the management of their oxen. Snyder was beating his cattle over the head with the butt end of his whip, when my father, returning on horse-back from a hunting trip, arrived and, appreciating the great importance of saving the remainder of the oxen, remonstrated with Snyder, telling him that they were our main dependence, and at the same time offering the assistance of our team. Snyder having taken offense at something Elliott had said declared that his team could pull up alone, and kept on using abusive language. Father tried to quiet the enraged man. Hard words followed. Then my father said: "We can settle this, John, when we get up the hill." "No," replied Snyder with an oath, "we will settle it now," and springing upon the tongue of a wagon, he struck my father a violent blow over the head with his heavy whip-stock. One blow followed another. Father was stunned for a moment and blinded by the blood streaming from the gashes in his head. Another blow was descending when my mother ran in between the men. Father saw the uplifted whip, but had only time to cry: "John, John," when down came the stroke upon mother. Quick as a thought my father's hunting knife was out and Snyder fell, fatally wounded. He was caught in the arms of W. C. Graves, carried up the hill-side, and laid

THE HUMBOLDT PALISADES. — THE HUMBOLDT SINK.

on the ground. My father regretted the act, and dashing the blood from his eyes went quickly to the assistance of the dying man. I can see him now, as he knelt over Snyder, trying to stanch the wound, while the blood from the gashes in his own head, trickling down his face, mingled with that of the dying man. In a few moments Snyder expired. Camp was pitched immediately, our wagon being some distance from the others. My father, anxious to do what he could for the dead, offered the boards of our wagon, from which to make a coffin. Then, coming to me, he said: "Daughter, do you think you can dress these wounds in my head? Your mother is not able, and they must be attended to." I answered by saying: "Yes, if you will tell me what to do." I brought a basin of water and sponge, and we went into the wagon, so that we might not be disturbed. When my work was at last finished, I burst out crying. Papa clasped me in his arms, saying: "I should not have asked so much of you," and talked to me until I controlled my feelings, so that we could go to the tent where mama was lying.

We then learned that trouble was brewing in the camp where Snyder's body lay. At the funeral my father stood sorrowfully by until the last clod was placed upon the grave. He and John Snyder had been good friends, and no one could have regretted the taking of that young life more than my father.

The members of the Donner party then held a council to decide upon the fate of my father, while we anxiously awaited the verdict. They refused to accept the plea of self-defense and decided that my father should be banished from the company and sent into the wilderness alone. It was a cruel sentence. And all this animosity towards my father was caused by Louis Keseburg, a German who had joined

our company away back on the plains. Keseburg was married to a young and pretty German girl, and used to abuse her, and was in the habit of beating her till she was black and blue. This aroused all the manhood in my father and he took Keseburg to task — telling him it must be stopped or measures would be taken to that effect. Keseburg did not dare to strike his wife again, but he hated my father and nursed his wrath until papa was so unfortunate as to have to take the life of a fellow-creature in self-defense. Then Keseburg's hour for revenge had come. But how a man like Keseburg, brutal and overbearing by nature, although highly educated, could have such influence over the company is more than I can tell. I have thought the subject over for hours but failed to arrive at a conclusion. The feeling against my father at one time was so strong that lynching was proposed. He was no coward and he bared his neck, saying, "Come on, gentlemen," but no one moved. It was thought more humane, perhaps, to send him into the wilderness to die of slow starvation or be murdered by the Indians; but my father did not die. God took care of him and his family, and at Donner Lake we seemed especially favored by the Almighty as not one of our family perished, and we were the only family no one member of which was forced to eat of human flesh to keep body and soul together. When the sentence of banishment was communicated to my father, he refused to go, feeling that he was justified before God and man, as he had only acted in self-defense.

Then came a sacrifice on the part of my mother. Knowing only too well what her life would be without him, yet fearful that if he remained he would meet with violence at the hands of his enemies, she implored him to go, but all to no avail until she urged him to remember the destitution of the company, saying that if he remained and escaped violence at their hands, he might nevertheless see his children starving and be helpless to aid them, while if he went on he could return and meet them with food. It was a fearful struggle; at last he consented, but not before he had secured a promise from the company to care for his wife and little ones.

My father was sent out into an unknown country without provisions or arms — even his horse was at first denied him. When we learned of this decision, I followed him through the darkness, taking Elliott with me, and carried him his rifle, pistols, ammunition and some food. I had determined to stay with him, and begged him to let me stay, but he would listen to no argument, saying that it was impossible. Finally, unclasping my arms from around him,

Plains of the Humboldt.

by Thomas Moran

30

THIRSTY OXEN STAMPEDING FOR WATER.

he placed me in charge of Elliott, who started back to camp with me—and papa was left alone. I had cried until I had hardly strength to walk, but when we reached camp and I saw the distress of my mother, with the little ones clinging around her and no arm to lean upon, it seemed suddenly to make a woman of me. I realized that I must be strong and help mama bear her sorrows.

We traveled on, but all life seemed to have left the party, and the hours dragged slowly along. Every day we would search for some sign of papa, who would leave a letter by the way-side in the top of a bush or in a split stick, and when he succeeded in killing geese or birds would scatter the feathers about so that we might know that he was not suffering for food. When possible, our fire would always be kindled on the spot where his had been. But a time came when we found no letter, and no trace of him. Had he starved by the way-side, or been murdered by the Indians?

My mother's despair was pitiful. Patty and I thought we would be bereft of her also. But

TRUCKEE MEADOWS. (RENO)

life and energy were again aroused by the danger that her children would starve. It was apparent that the whole company would soon be put on a short allowance of food, and the snow-capped mountains gave an ominous hint of the fate that really befell us in the Sierra. Our wagon was found to be too heavy, and was abandoned with everything we could spare, and the remaining things were packed in part of another wagon. We had two horses left from the wreck, which could hardly drag themselves along, but they managed to carry my two little brothers. The rest of us had to walk, one going beside the horse to hold on my youngest brother who was only two and a half years of age. The Donners were not with us when my father was

banished, but were several days in advance of our train. Walter Herron, one of our drivers, who was traveling with the Donners, left the wagons and joined my father.

On the 19th of October, while traveling along the Truckee, our hearts were gladdened by the return of Stanton, with seven mules loaded with provisions. Mr. McClutchen was ill and could not travel, but Captain Sutter had sent two of his Indian vaqueros, Luis and Salvador with Stanton. Hungry as we were, Stanton brought us something better than food—news that my father was alive. Stanton had met him not far from Sutter's Fort; he had been three days without food, and his horse was not able to carry him. Stanton had given him a horse and some provis-

TRUCKEE CAÑON.

32

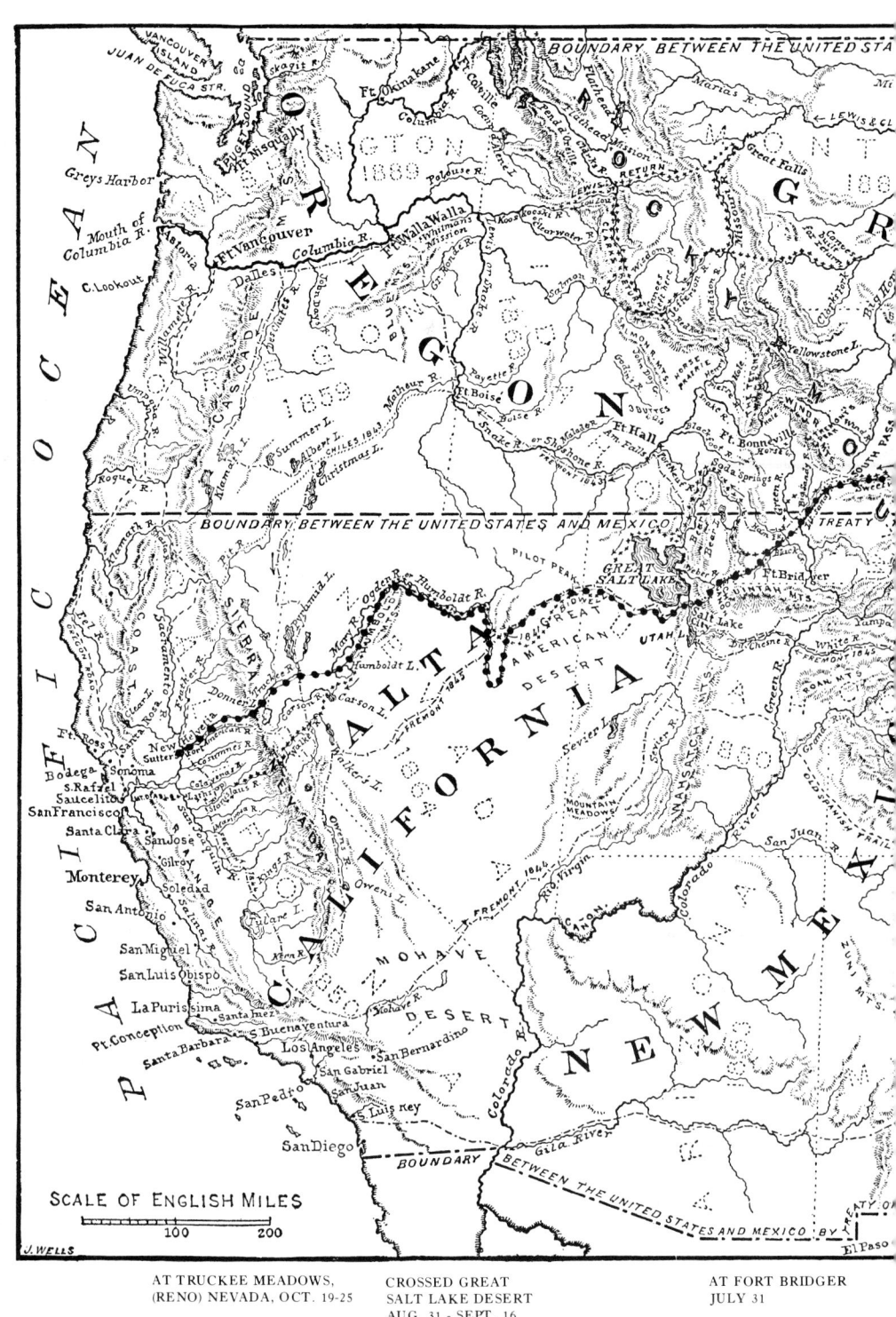

AT TRUCKEE MEADOWS,
(RENO) NEVADA, OCT. 19-25

ARRIVED DONNER LAKE, CALIFORNIA
OCT. 31

CROSSED GREAT
SALT LAKE DESERT
AUG. 31 - SEPT. 16

AT FORT BRIDGER
JULY 31

SIGNIFICANT DATES IN THE DONNER PARTY'S 1846 TREK

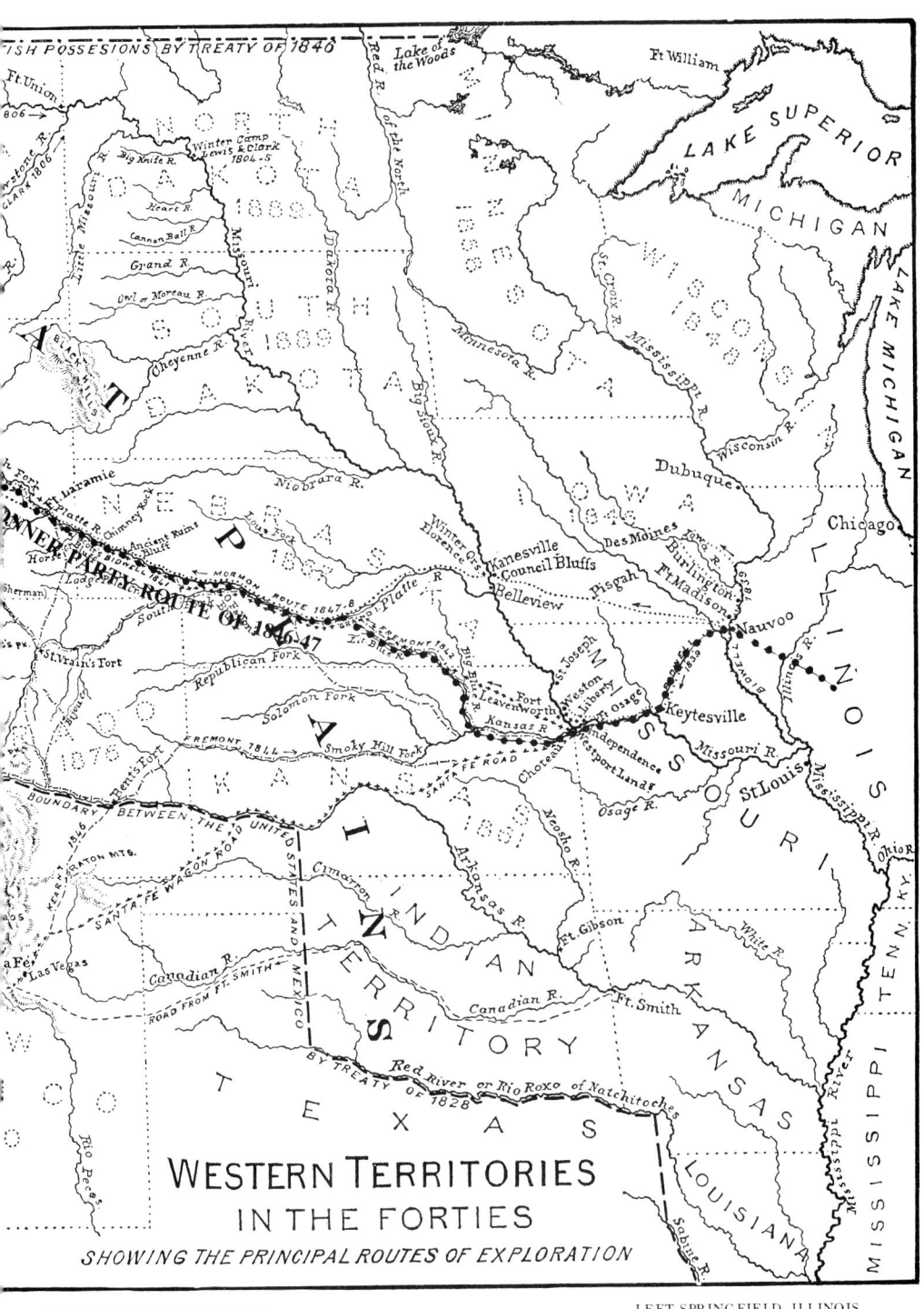

WESTERN TERRITORIES IN THE FORTIES

SHOWING THE PRINCIPAL ROUTES OF EXPLORATION

AT FORT LARAMIE, WYOMING
JULY 4

LEFT SPRINGFIELD, ILLINOIS
APRIL 14

ACROSS THE PLAINS ARE GIVEN ALONG THE BOTTOM OF THE MAP.

TRUCKEE RIVER CANYON
BY THOMAS MORAN

DONNER LAKE, FROM THE OLD SACRAMENTO TRAIL.

ions and he had gone on. We now packed what little we had left on one mule and started with Stanton. My mother rode on a mule, carrying Tommy in her lap; Patty and Jim rode behind the two Indians, and I behind Mr. Stanton, and in this way we journeyed on through the rain, looking up with fear towards the mountains, where snow was already falling although it was only the last week in October. Winter had set in a month earlier than usual. All trails and roads were covered; and our only guide was the summit which it seemed we would never reach. Despair drove many nearly frantic. Each family tried to cross the mountains but found it impossible. When it was seen that the wagons could not be dragged through the snow, their goods and provisions were packed on oxen and another start was made, men and women walking in the snow up to their waists, carrying their children in their arms and trying to drive their cattle. The Indians said they could find no road, so a halt was called, and Stanton went ahead with the guides, and came back and reported that we could get across if we kept right on, but that it would be impossible if snow fell. He was in favor of a forced march until the other side of the summit should be reached, but some of our party were so tired and exhausted with the day's labor that they declared they could not take another step; so the few who knew the danger that the night might bring yielded to the many, and we camped within three miles of the summit.

That night came the dreaded snow. Around the camp-fires under the trees great feathery flakes came whirling down. The air was so full of them that one could see objects only a few feet away. The Indians knew we were doomed, and one of them wrapped his blanket about him and stood all night under a tree. We children slept soundly on our cold bed of snow with a soft white mantle falling over us so thickly that every few moments my mother would have to shake the shawl — our only covering — to keep us from being buried alive. In the morning the snow lay deep on mountain and valley. With heavy hearts we turned back to a cabin that had been built by the Murphy-Schallenberger party two years before. We built more cabins and prepared as best we could for the winter. That camp, which proved the camp of death to many in our company, was made on the shore of a lake, since known as "Donner Lake." The Donners were camped in Alder Creek Valley below the lake, and were, if possible, in a worse condition than ourselves.

ON THE WAY TO THE SUMMIT.

CAMP AT DONNER LAKE, NOVEMBER, 1846.

The snow came on so suddenly that they had no time to build cabins, but hastily put up brush sheds, covering them with pine boughs.

Three double cabins were built at Donner Lake, which were known as the " Breen Cabin," the " Murphy Cabin," and the " Reed-Graves Cabin." The cattle were all killed, and the meat was placed in snow for preservation. My mother had no cattle to kill, but she made arrangements for some, promising to give two for one in California. Stanton and the Indians made their home in my mother's cabin.

Many attempts were made to cross the mountains, but all who tried were driven back by the pitiless storms. Finally a party was organized, since known as the " Forlorn Hope." They made snow-shoes, and fifteen started, ten men and five women, but only seven lived to reach California; eight men perished. They were over a month on the way, and the horrors endured by that Forlorn Hope no pen can describe nor imagination conceive. The noble Stanton was one of the party, and perished the sixth day out, thus sacrificing his life for strangers. I can find no words in which to express a fitting tribute to the memory of Stanton.

The misery endured during those four months at Donner Lake in our little dark cabins under the snow would fill pages and make the coldest heart ache. Christmas was near, but to the starving its memory gave no comfort. It came and passed without observance, but my mother had determined weeks before that her children should have a treat on this one day. She had laid away a few dried apples, some beans, a bit of tripe, and a small piece of bacon. When this hoarded store was brought out, the delight of the little ones knew no bounds. The cooking was watched carefully, and when we sat down to our Christmas dinner mother said, " Children, eat slowly, for this one day you can have all you wish." So bitter was the misery relieved by that one bright day, that I have never since sat down to a Christmas dinner without my thoughts going back to Donner Lake.

The storms would often last ten days at a time, and we would have to cut chips from the logs inside which formed our cabins, in order to start a fire. We could scarcely walk, and the men had hardly strength to procure wood. We would drag ourselves through the snow from one cabin to another, and some mornings snow would have to be shoveled out of the fireplace before a fire could be made. Poor little children were crying with hunger, and mothers were cry-

38

ing because they had so little to give their children. We seldom thought of bread, we had been without it so long. Four months of such suffering would fill the bravest hearts with despair.

During the closing days of December, 1846, gold was found in my mother's cabin at Donner Lake by John Denton. I remember the night well. The storm fiends were shrieking in their wild mirth, we were sitting about the fire in our little dark home, busy with our thoughts. Denton with his cane kept knocking pieces off the large rocks used as fire-irons on which to place the wood. Something bright attracted his attention, and picking up pieces of the rock he examined them closely; then turning to my mother he said, " Mrs. Reed, this is gold." My mother replied that she wished it were bread. Denton knocked more chips from the rocks, and he hunted in the ashes for the shining particles until he had gathered about a teaspoonful. This he tied in a small piece of buckskin and placed in his pocket, saying, " If we ever get away from here I am coming back for more." Denton started out with the first relief party but perished on the way, and no one thought of the gold in his pocket. Denton was about thirty years of age; he was born in Sheffield, England, and was a gunsmith and gold-beater by trade. Gold has never been found on the shore of the lake, but a few miles from there in the mountain cañons, from which this rock possibly came, rich mines have been discovered.

Time dragged slowly along till we were no longer on short allowance but were simply starving. My mother determined to make an effort to cross the mountains. She could not see her children die without trying to get them food. It was hard to leave them but she felt that it must be done. She told them she would bring them bread, so they were willing to stay, and with no guide but a compass we started—my mother, Eliza, Milt Elliott and myself. Milt wore snow shoes and we followed in his tracks. We were five days in the mountains; Eliza gave out the first day and had to return, but we kept on and climbed one high mountain after another only to see others higher still ahead. Often I would have to crawl up the mountains, being too tired to walk. The nights were made hideous by the screams of wild beasts heard in the distance. Again, we would be lulled to sleep by the moan of the pine trees, which seemed to sympathize with our loneliness. One morning we awoke to find ourselves in a well of snow. During the night, while in the deep sleep of exhaustion, the heat of the fire had melted the snow and our little camp had gradually sunk many feet below the surface until we were literally buried in a well of snow. The danger was that any attempt to get out might bring an avalanche

THE CAMP OF DEATH.

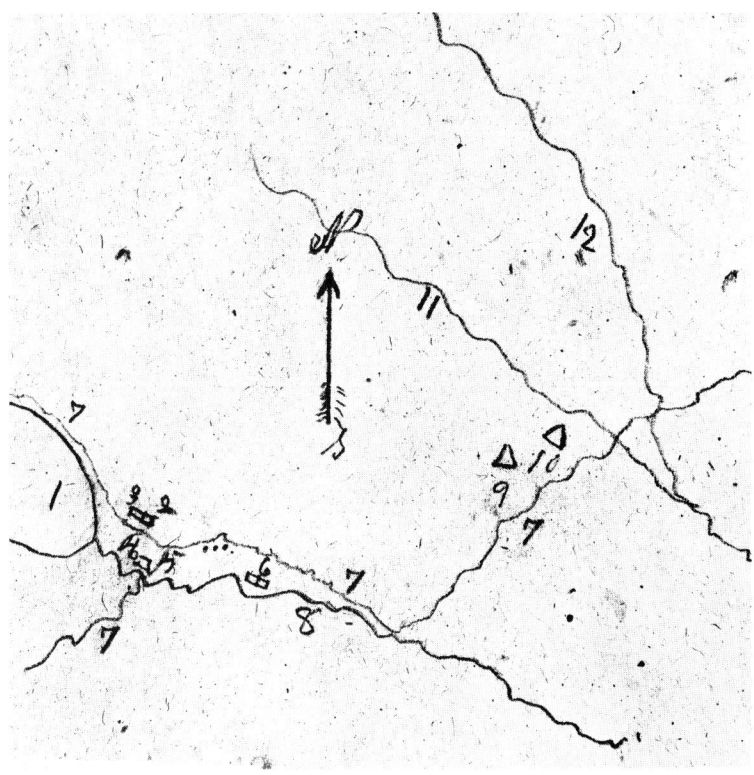

1. Lake
2. Old Cabin
3. Keseberg's addition
4. Big Rock
5. Murphy's Cabin

6. Grave's Cabin
7. Roads
8. Donner Creek
9, 10. Donner tents
11, 12. Creeks

MAP OF DONNER PARTY CAMPS BY SURVIVOR W.C. GRAVES, 18 YEARS OLD IN 1847.

40

upon us, but finally steps were carefully made and we reached the surface. My foot was badly frozen, so we were compelled to return, and just in time, for that night a storm came on, the most fearful of the winter, and we should have perished had we not been in the cabins.

We now had nothing to eat but raw hides and they were on the roof of the cabin to keep out the snow; when prepared for cooking and boiled they were simply a pot of glue. When the hides were taken off our cabin and we were left without shelter Mr. Breen gave us a home with his family, and Mrs. Breen prolonged my life by slipping me little bits of meat now and then when she discovered that I could not eat the hide. Death had already claimed many in our party and it seemed as though relief never would reach us. Baylis Williams, who had been in delicate health before we left Springfield, was the first to die; he passed away before starvation had really set in.

I am a Catholic although my parents were not. I often went to the Catholic church before leaving home, but it was at Donner Lake that I made the vow to be a Catholic. The Breens were the only Catholic family in the Donner party and prayers were said aloud regularly in that cabin night and morning. Our only light was from little pine sticks split up like kin-dling wood and kept constantly on the hearth. I was very fond of kneeling by the side of Mr. Breen and holding these little torches so that he might see to read. One night we had all gone to bed — I was with my mother and the little ones, all huddled together to keep from freezing — but I could not sleep. It was a fearful night and I felt that the hour was not far distant when we would go to sleep — never to wake again in this world. All at once I found myself on my knees with my hands clasped, looking up through the darkness, making a vow that if God would send us relief and let me see my father again I would be a Catholic. That prayer was answered.

On his arrival at Sutter's Fort, my father made known the situation of the emigrants, and Captain Sutter offered at once to do everything possible for their relief. He furnished horses and provisions and my father and Mr. McClutchen started for the mountains, coming as far as possible with horses and then with packs on their backs proceeding on foot; but they were finally compelled to return. Captain Sutter was not surprised at their defeat. He stated that there were no able-bodied men in that vicinity, all having gone down the country with Frémont to fight the Mexicans. He advised my father to go to

ARRIVAL OF THE FIRST RELIEF PARTY ON FEBRUARY 19, 1847

YERBA BUENA (SAN FRANCISCO) IN MARCH, 1847.

Yerba Buena, now San Francisco, and make his case known to the naval officer in command. My father was in fact conducting parties there — when the seven members of the Forlorn Hope arrived from across the mountains. Their famished faces told the story. Cattle were killed and men were up all night drying beef and making flour by hand mills, nearly 200 pounds being made in one night, and a party of seven, commanded by Captain Reasen P. Tucker, were sent to our relief by Captain Sutter and the alcalde, Mr. Sinclair. On the evening of February 19th, 1847, they reached our cabins, where all were starving. They shouted to attract attention. Mr. Breen, clambered up the icy steps from our cabin, and soon we heard the blessed words, "Relief, thank God, relief!" There was joy at Donner Lake that night, for we did not know the fate of the Forlorn Hope and we were told that relief parties would come and go until all were across the mountains. But with the joy sorrow was strangely blended. There were tears in other eyes than those of children; strong men sat down and wept. For the dead were lying about on the snow, some even unburied, since

the living had not had strength to bury their dead. When Milt Elliott died,— our faithful friend, who seemed so like a brother,— my mother and I dragged him up out of the cabin and covered him with snow. Commencing at his feet, I patted the pure white snow down softly until I reached his face. Poor Milt! it was hard to cover that face from sight forever, for with his death our best friend was gone.

On the 22d of February the first relief started with a party of twenty-three — men, women and children. My mother and her family were among the number. It was a bright sunny morning and we felt happy, but we had not gone far when Patty and Tommy gave out. They were not able to stand the fatigue and it was not thought safe to allow them to proceed, so Mr. Glover informed mama that they would have to be sent back to the cabins to await the next expedition. What language can express our feelings? My mother said that she would go back with her children — that we would all go back together. This the relief party would not permit, and Mr. Glover promised mama that as soon as they reached Bear Valley he himself would return for her chil-

DIARY OF PATRICK BREEN
(February 6-8, 1847)

Satd 6th it snowed faster last night & today than it has done this winter & still Continues without an intermission wind S.W. Murphys folks or Keysburgs say they cant eat hides. I wish we had enough of them Mrs. Eddy very weak

Sund. 7th Ceased to snow last [night] after one of the most Severe Storms we experienced this winter the snow fell about 4 feet deep I had to shovel the snow off our shanty this morning it thawed so fast & thawed during the whole storm. today it is quite pleasant wind S.W. Milt here today says Mrs. Reid has to get a hide from Mrs. Murphy & McCutchins child died 2nd of this month.

Mond 8th fine clear morning wind S.W. froze hard last [night] Spitzer died last night about 3 o clock to [day?] we will bury him in the snow Mrs. Eddy died on the night of the 7th.

MRS. BRINN IN TRIBULATION.

dren. Finally my mother, turning to Mr. Glover said, "Are you a Mason?" He replied that he was. "Will you promise me on the word of a Mason that if we do not meet their father you will return and save my children?" He pledged himself that he would. My father was a member of the Mystic Tie and mama had great faith in the word of a Mason. It was a sad parting — a fearful struggle. The men turned aside, not being able to hide their tears. Patty said, "I want to see papa, but I will take good care of Tommy and I do not want you to come back." Mr. Glover returned with the children and, providing them with food, left them in the care of Mr. Breen.

With sorrowful hearts we traveled on, walking through the snow in single file. The men wearing snow-shoes broke the way and we followed in their tracks. At night we lay down on the snow to sleep, to awake to find our clothing all frozen, even to our shoe-strings. At break of day we were again on the road, owing to the fact that we could make better time over the frozen snow. The sunshine, which it would seem would have been welcome, only added to our misery. The dazzling reflection of the snow was very trying to the eyes, while its heat melted our frozen clothing, making them cling to our bodies. My brother was too small to step in the tracks made by the men, and in order to travel he had to place his knee on the little hill of snow after each step and climb over. Mother coaxed him along, telling him that every step he took he was getting nearer papa and nearer something to eat. He was the youngest child that walked over the Sierra Nevada. On our second day's journey John Denton gave out and declared it would be impossible for him to travel, but he begged his companions to continue their journey. A fire was built and he was left lying on a bed of freshly cut pine boughs, peacefully smoking. He looked so comfortable that my little brother wanted to stay with him; but when the second relief party reached him poor Denton was past waking. His last thoughts seemed to have gone back to his childhood's home, as a little poem was found by his side, the pencil apparently just dropped from his hand.

Captain Tucker's party on their way to the cabins had lightened their packs of a sufficient quantity of provisions to supply the sufferers

DONNER LAKE   BY THOMAS MORAN

on their way out. But when we reached the place where the cache had been made by hanging the food on a tree, we were horrified to find that wild animals had destroyed it, and again starvation stared us in the face. But my father was hurrying over the mountains, and met us in our hour of need with his hands full of bread. He had expected to meet us on this day, and had stayed up all night baking bread to give us. He brought with him fourteen men. Some of his party were ahead, and when they saw us coming they called out, "Is Mrs. Reed with you? If she is, tell her Mr. Reed is here." We heard the call; mother knelt on the snow, while I tried to run to meet papa.

When my father learned that two of his children were still at the cabins, he hurried on, so fearful was he that they might perish before he reached them. He seemed to fly over the snow, and made in two days the distance we had been five in traveling, and was overjoyed to find Patty and Tommy alive. He reached Donner Lake on the first of March, and what a sight met his gaze! The fam-

ished little children and the death-like look of all made his heart ache. He filled Patty's apron with biscuits, which she carried around, giving one to each person. He had soup made for the infirm, and rendered every assistance possible to the sufferers. Leaving them with about seven days' provisions, he started out with a party of seventeen, all that were able to travel. Three of his men were left at the cabins to procure wood and assist the helpless. My father's party (the second relief) had not traveled many miles when a storm broke upon them. With the snow came a perfect hurricane. The crying of half-frozen children, the lamenting of the mothers, and the suffering of the whole party was heart-rending; and above all could be heard the shrieking of the storm King. One who has never witnessed a blizzard in the Sierra can form no idea of the situation. All night my father and his men worked unceasingly through the raging storm, trying to erect shelter for the dying women and children. At times the hurricane would burst forth with such violence that he felt

LEAVING THE WEAK TO DIE.

MEETING OF PATTY AND HER FATHER

alarmed on account of the tall timber surrounding the camp. The party were destitute of food, all supplies that could be spared having been left with those at the cabins. The relief party had cached provisions on their way over to the cabins, and my father had sent three of the men forward for food before the storm set in; but they could not return. Thus, again, death stared all in the face. At one time the fire was nearly gone; had it been lost, all would have perished. Three days and nights they were exposed to the fury of the elements. Finally my father became snow-blind and could do no more, and he would have died but for the exertions of William McClutchen and Hiram Miller, who worked over him all night. From this time forward, the toil and responsibility rested upon McClutchen and Miller.

The storm at last ceased, and these two determined to set out over the snow and send back relief to those not able to travel. Hiram Miller picked up Tommy and started. Patty thought she could walk, but gradually everything faded from her sight, and she too seemed to be dying. All other sufferings were now forgotten, and everything was done to revive the child. My father found some crumbs in the thumb of his woolen mitten; warming and moistening them between his own lips, he gave them to her and thus saved her life, and afterward she was carried along by different ones in the company. Patty was not alone in her travels. Hidden away in her bosom was a tiny doll, which she had carried day and night through all of our trials. Sitting before a nice, bright fire at Woodworth's

JOHN A. SUTTER

BY THOMAS MORAN

SUMMIT OF THE SIERRAS.

48

PATTY'S DOLL

Camp, she took dolly out to have a talk, and told her of all her new happiness.

There was untold suffering at that "Starved Camp," as the place has since been called. When my father reached Woodworth's Camp, a third relief started in at once and rescued the living. A fourth relief went on to Donner Lake, as many were still there — and many remain there still, including George Donner and wife, Jacob Donner and wife and four of their children. George Donner had met with an accident which rendered him unable to travel; and his wife would not leave him to die alone. It would take pages to tell of the heroic acts and noble deeds of those who lie sleeping about Donner Lake.

Most of the survivors, when brought in from the mountains, were taken by the different relief parties to Sutter's Fort, and the generous hearted captain did everything possible for the sufferers. Out of the eighty-three persons who were snowed in at Donner Lake, forty-two perished, and of the thirty-one emigrants who left Springfield, Illinois, that spring morning, only eighteen lived to reach California. Alcalde Sinclair took my mother and her family to his own home, and we were surrounded with every comfort. Mrs. Sinclair was the dearest of women. Never can I forget their kindness. But our anxiety was not over, for we knew that my father's party had been caught in the

VIEW OF CAPTAIN SUTTER'S FORT NEAR SACRAMENTO CITY, CALIFORNIA, 1846.

Tall stumps at site of Donner camp at Alder Creek, indicating approximate depth of snow when cut.

Starvation Camp.—Stumps cut by the Donner Lake Party, 1846.
(From photograph published in 1872.)

Before leaving Donner Lake with a rescue party, Mrs. Graves cached her gold coins. But a few days later she died while crossing the mountains, and the secret passed with her. Her lost hoard was discovered on the north shore of the lake in 1891. Below, Mrs. Graves' cache.

storm. I can see my mother now, as she stood leaning against the door for hours at a time, looking towards the mountains. At last my father arrived at Mr. Sinclair's with the little ones, and our family were again united. That day's happiness repaid us for much that we had suffered; and it was spring in California.

Words cannot tell how beautiful the spring appeared to us coming out of the mountains from that long winter at Donner Lake in our little dark cabins under the snow. Before us now lay, in all its beauty, the broad valley of the Sacramento. I remember one day, when traveling down Napa Valley, we stopped at noon to have lunch under the shade of an oak; but I was not hungry; I was too full of the beautiful around me to think of eating. So I wandered off by myself to a lovely little knoll and stood there in a bed of wild flowers, looking up and down the green valley, all dotted with trees. The birds were singing with very joy in the branches over my head, and the blessed sun was smiling down upon all as though in benediction. I drank it in for a moment, and then began kissing my hand and wafting kisses to Heaven in thanksgiving to the Almighty for creating a world so beautiful. I felt so near God at that moment that it seemed to me I could feel His breath warm on my cheek. By and by I heard papa calling, " Daughter, where are you ? Come, child, we are ready to start, and you have had no lunch," I ran and caught him by the hand, saying, " Buy this place, please, and let us make our home here." He stood looking around for a moment, and said, " It *is* a lovely spot," and then we passed on.

THE END

INDEPENDENCE ROCK, SWEETWATER RIVER.

52

Know all men by these presents that I James F Reed and Hiram O. Miller, are held and firmly bound unto the heirs. of the Estate of Jacob Donner, deceased in the full sum. of Six Hundred Dollars. for the payment of which will and truly to be made we bind Our selves Our heirs Executors and administrators jointly by these presents,

Given Under Our hands and seals. this 12th day of May A D 1847.

Now Know Ye that the Conditions of the above Obligation is Such that where as the said James F Reed has this day been duly appointed administrator of the Estate of Jacob Donner deceased as Well as guardian of George Donner and Mary Donner Orphans: who are minors under the age of Twenty one Years,

Now if the said James F Reed shall well and truly discharge the duties of the said office then and in such Case, the above obligation Shall be void and Null, otherwise to remain in full force and

Attest
[signature]

James F Reed Seal
Hiram C Miller Seal

Oath of James F. Reed, dated May 12, 1847, to serve as guardian of George Donner and Mary Donner, orphans of Jacob Donner.

Donner Lake, just 22 years after that fateful winter, was served by the transcontinental railroad in 1869. In this 1879 view, wagon road, telegraph, and hotel were also present. Note, however, the snowsheds on the rail line (upper part of view) and the steep pitches of roofs designed to cope with the severe snowfalls here.

The face of this rock formed the north end and the fireplace of the Murphy cabin. General Stephen W. Kearny, on June 22, 1847, buried under the middle of the cabin the bodies found in the vicinity. The plaque bears the names of the members of the Donner Party.

THE DONNER PARTY

FAMILY GROUPS   **DEATHS**

BREEN-DOLAN — (four wagons). From Keokuk, Iowa, Patrick and Margaret Breen, both 40; their seven children, John, 14; Edward, 13; Patrick, Jr., 11; Simon, 9; Peter, 7; James, 4; Isabella, 1. Patrick Dolan, 40, of Keokuk. *The entire Breen family survived. Dolan perished with the snowshoe party.*   1

DONNER — (six wagons). From Springfield, Ill, George, 62, and Tamsen Donner, 45; their three children, Frances, 6; Georgia, 4; Eliza, 3. Donner's daughters by a previous marriage, Elitha, 14, and Leanna, 12. *All five girls survived; George died at Alder Creek and Tamsen at the lake camp.*   2

From Springfield, Ill., Jacob, 65, and Elizabeth Donner, 45; their five children, George, 9; Mary, 7; Isaac, 5; Samuel, 4; Lewis, 3. Elizabeth Donner's sons by a previous marriage, Solomon, 14, and William Hook, 12. *The parents, Samuel, and Lewis died at Alder Creek; Isaac Donner and William Hook perished with the relief parties.*   6

Employees — Noah James, 20; Samuel Shoemaker, 25. *Shoemaker died at Alder Creek.*   1

EDDY — (one wagon). From Belleville, Ill., William H., 28, and Eleanor Eddy, 25; their two children, James, 3, and Margaret, 1. *Mrs. Eddy and the children died at the lake camp.*   3

GRAVES-FOSDICK — (three wagons). Franklin Graves, Sr., 57, and Elizabeth Graves, 47; their nine children, Mary, 20; William, 18; Eleanor, 15; Lovina, 13; Nancy, 9; Jonathan, 7; Franklin Ward Graves, Jr., 5; Elizabeth, 1; Sarah, 22, and her husband Jay Fosdick, 23. *Franklin Graves, Sr., and Fosdick died with the snowshoe party. Mrs. Graves and Franklin Ward Graves, Jr., died witn the relief parties. The baby Elizabeth died after reaching Sutter's Fort.*   5

Employee — John Snyder, 25, *slain in knife fight with Reed.*   1

KESEBERG — (two wagons). From Berleburg, Westphalia, Germany, by way of Ohio, Louis, 32, and Philippine Keseberg, 23; their two children, Ada, 3, and Louis, Jr., 1. *Louis, Jr., perished at the lake camp, and Ada died with a relief party.*   2

Employee — Karl Burger, 30, from Germany; *died at the lake camp.*   1

McCUTCHEN — (no wagons). From Missouri, William, 30, and Amanda McCutchen, 24; their child, Harriet, 1. *The baby died at the lake camp.*   1

MURPHY-FOSTER-PIKE — (two wagons). From Tennessee and St. Louis, Lavina Murphy, 50; her seven children, Landrum, 15; Mary, 13; Lemuel, 12; William, 11; Simon, 10; Sarah, 23, her husband William M. Foster, 28, and their child, George, 4; Harriet, 21, her husband William M. Pike, 25, and their children, Naomi, 3, and Catherine, 1. *Mrs. Murphy, Landrum, Catherine Pike, and George Foster died at the lake camp. Lemuel perished with the snowshoers. Pike was shot to death accidentally.*   6

REED — (Three wagons). From Springfield, Ill., James Frazier, 46, and Margaret Reed, 32; their three children, Martha (Patty), 8; James, Jr., 5; Thomas, 3; and Virginia Backenstoe Reed, 13, Mrs. Reed's daughter by previous marriage; also Sarah Keyes, Mrs. Reed's mother. *Sarah Keyes died on the trail in Kansas; otherwise the entire Reed family survived.*   1

Employees — Milton Elliott, 28; Walter Herron, 25; James Smith, 25; Baylis Williams, 24; his half-sister, Eliza Williams, 25. *Elliott and Williams died at the lake camp, Smith at Alder Creek.*   3

WOLFINGER — (one wagon). From Germany, Mr. and Mrs. Wolfinger, about the age of the Kesebergs. *Wolfinger apparently slain by Reinhardt and Spitzer.*   1

INDIVIDUALS

ANTONIO, a young herder from New Mexico, traveling with Donners and Reeds. *Perished with snowshoers.*   1

JOHN DENTON, 28, Sheffield, England, traveling with Donners. *Died with relief party.*   1

LUKE HALLORAN, 25, Missouri, traveling with Donners; *died after party's escape from Wasatch Mountains.*   1

HARDCOOP, past 60, a Belgian from Cincinnati, traveling with Kesebergs. *Left to die on desert.*   1

LUIS AND SALVADOR, Indians from Sutter's Fort. *Members of snowshoe party shot to death by Foster.*   2

AUGUSTUS SPITZER AND JOSEPH REINHARDT, about 30, from Germany; one wagon. *Spitzer perished at lake camp, Reinhardt at Alder Creek.*   2

CHARLES TYLER STANTON, 35, Chicago, traveling with Donners. *Died with snowshoers.*   1

JEAN BAPTISTE TRUBODE, a young teamster from New Mexico, picked up by Donners.   0

SURVIVED, 47; PERISHED, 43.

ROSTER OF LIFE

Ages are given in parentheses for individuals who were children in 1847, even though their portraits show them as adults. Sex is indicated (M or F) for adults.

SURVIVORS WHO LEFT THE TRAIN EARLY

Walter Herron. (M)   William McCutcheon. (M)
Hiram Miller. (M)

SURVIVOR OF BANISHMENT
James F. Reed. (M)

James F. Reed

Mary Graves

SURVIVORS OF THE EXPEDITION OF FORLORN HOPE (SNOWSHOE PARTY-DECEMBER)

William H. Eddy. (M)   Sarah Murphy Foster. (F)
William Foster. (M)   Harriet Murphy Pike. (F)
Amanda McCutcheon. (F)   Sarah Graves Fosdick. (F)
Mary Graves (F)

Mrs. Margaret W. Reed

W.C. Graves

SURVIVORS OF THE FIRST RELIEF EXPEDITION (FEBRUARY)

Mrs. Margaret Reed. (F)   Simon Breen. (9)
James Reed Jr. (5)   Mary Murphy. (13)
Virginia Reed. (12)   William Murphy. (11)
George Donner, Jr. (9)   Naomi Pike. (3)
Elitha Donner. (14)   Mrs. Phillipine Keseberg. (F)
Leanna Donner. (12)   William Graves (M)
Eliza Williams. (F)   Mrs. Wolfinger (F)
Noah James. (M)   Lovina Graves. (13)
Edward Breen. (13)   Eleanor Graves. (15)

Patty Reed

Georgia Donner

SURVIVORS OF THE SECOND RELIEF EXPEDITION (EARLY MARCH)

Patrick Breen (M)   Margaret Breen (F)
Solomon Hook. (14)   John Breen (14)
Mary Donner (7)   Patrick Breen, Jr. (11)
Patty Reed (8)   James Breen (4)
Thomas Reed. (3)   Peter Breen (7)
Patrick Breen. (M)   Jonathan Graves. (7)
Isabella Breen. (1)   Elizabeth Graves (Jr.). (1)
Nancy Graves. (9)   (died at Sutter's Fort)

Lewis Keseberg

Eliza Donner

SURVIVORS OF THE THIRD RELIEF EXPEDITION (MID-MARCH)

Simon Murphy (10)   Georgia Donner (4)
Frances Donner. (6)   Eliza Donner (3)
John Baptiste Trubode. (M)

Patrick Breen

John Breen

SURVIVOR OF THE FOURTH RELIEF EXPEDITION (MID-APRIL)

Lewis Keseberg (M)

Margaret Breen

Edward Breen

Peter Breen

James Breen

Patrick Breen Jr.

Isabella Breen

Simon Breen

ROSTER OF DEATH

Ages are given in parentheses for individuals who were children in 1847. Sex is indicated (M or F) for adults.

Of the 23 men, 15 women, and 41 children who reached Donner Lake; over 2/3 of the men died (and most died early), about 1/3 of the children died (beginning in the middle of the ordeal), but just 1/4 of the women (or 4) died (and most died near the end of the entrapment). Were the men inspired by the heroics of the age and by their natural impatience to over-exertion? Were food portions doled out equally in spite of size? Or was the reason physiological? Or was it psychological?

ON THE TRAIL

Sarah Keyes. (F)   Mr. Hardcoop. (M)
Luke Halloran. (M)   Mr. Wolfinger. (M)
John Snyder. (M)   William N. Pike. (M)

AT THE DONNER LAKE-ALDER CREEK CAMPS IN DECEMBER

Jacob Donner. (M)   Samuel Shoemaker. (M)
Baylis Williams. (M)   Joseph Rhinehart. (M)
James Smith. (M)   Charles Burger. (M)

Charles Stanton

ON THE EXPEDITION OF THE FORLORN HOPE (SNOWSHOE PARTY-DECEMBER)

Charles Stanton. (M)   Lemuel Murphy. (12)
Jay Fosdick. (M)   Antonio. (M)
Patrick Dolan. (M)   Luis. (M)
Franklin Graves, Sr. (M) Salvador. (M)

AT THE DONNER LAKE-ALDER CREEK CAMPS IN JANUARY AND FEBRUARY

Landrum Murphy. (15)   Augustus Spitzer. (M)
Lewis Keseberg Jr. (1)   Milton Elliott. (M)
Eleanor Eddy. (F)   Harriet McCutcheon. (1)
Margaret Eddy. (1)   Catherine Pike. (1)

ON THE FIRST RELIEF EXPEDITION (FEBRUARY)

William Hook. (12)   Ada Keseberg. (3)
John Denton. (M)

AT THE DONNER LAKE-ALDER CREEK CAMPS IN MARCH

George Foster. (4)   Lewis Donner. (3)
James P. Eddy. (3)   Samuel Donner. (4)
Elizabeth Donner. (F)   Lavina Murphy. (F)
George Donner. (M)   Tamsen Donner. (F)

ON THE SECOND RELIEF EXPEDITION (EARLY MARCH)

Mrs. Elizabeth Graves (F)   Franklin Ward Graves Jr. (5)
Isaac Donner. (5)

ON THE THIRD AND FOURTH RELIEF EXPEDITIONS

no deaths

AT SUTTER'S FORT

Elizabeth Graves. (1)

ROSTER OF RELIEF PARTIES

MEMBERS OF FIRST RELIEF

Aquila Glover.
R. Moutrey.

Joseph Sells.
John Rhodes.
Daniel Rhodes.

Captain Reasin P. Tucker.
Edward Coffeymire.

SECOND RELIEF

James Reed.
Hiram Miller.
Britt Greenwood.

Howard Oakley.
Charles Stone.
John Turner.
Matthew Dofar.

Charles Cady.
Nicholas Clark.
William McCutchen.

(Selim E. Woodworth, Joseph Gendreau and others went partway and guarded supplies in camp.)

Nicholas Clark

Reasin P. Tucker

William McCutchen

THIRD RELIEF

James P. Eddy.
William Foster.

John Stark.
William Thompson.
Howard Oakley.

Hiram Miller.
Charles Stone.

FOURTH RELIEF

Captain Fallon.
Captain Reasin P. Tucker.

John Rhodes.
Edward Coffeymire.

Keyser.
Jo Foster.

Running gear of a Donner Party wagon abandoned in Great Salt Lake Desert

Part of the running gears of a wagon abandoned in the Salt Desert. Crater Island to the left; Silver Island in the distance. Note the trail of the emigrant wagons still preserved in the salt.

Ruts made by the emigrant wagons of 1846 still preserved in the Salt Desert near Crater Island (looking east).

Hub of emigrant wagon abandoned in the salt.

Remains of what was probably James F. Reed's "Pioneer Palace Car," abandoned in the Salt Desert in 1846. The hubs of three wheels are visible in this photograph.

Track of Donner Party across Great Salt Lake Desert, oxen bones, and abandoned wagons.

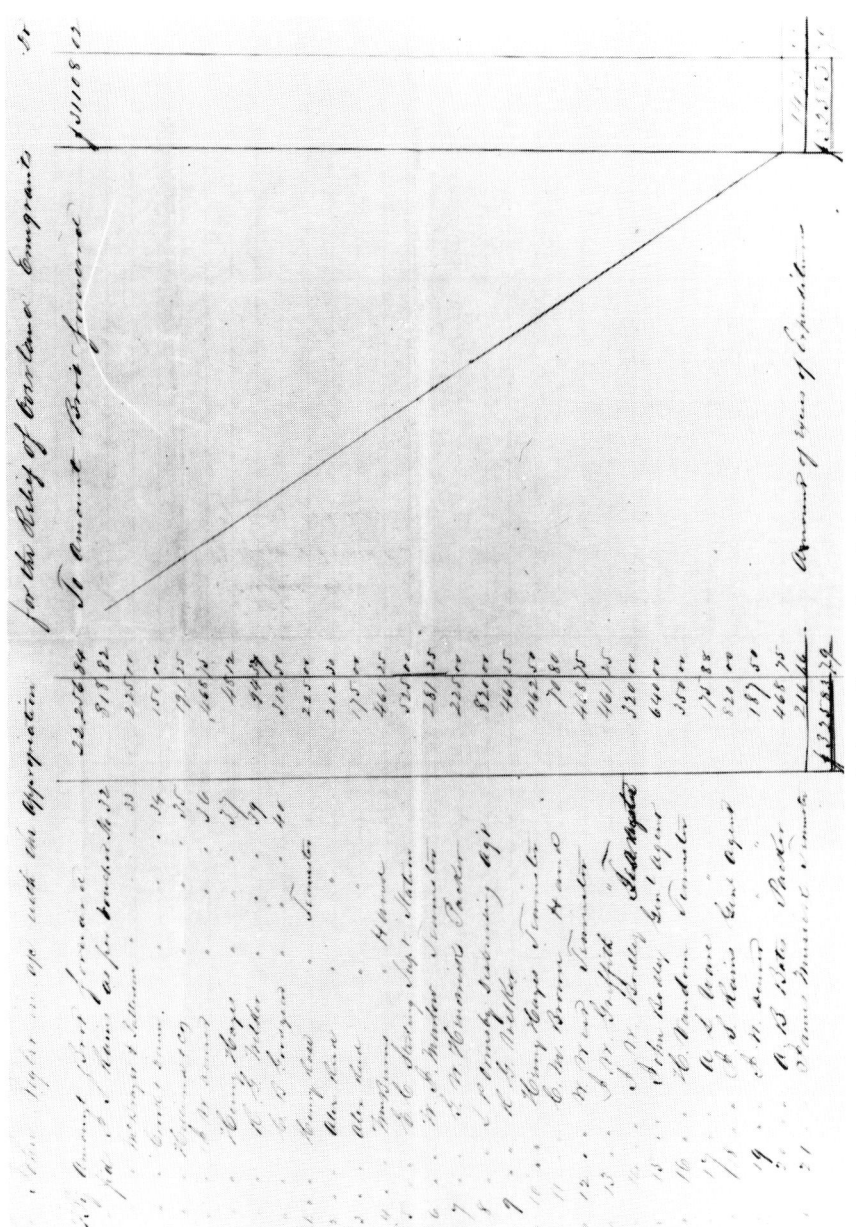

A page from the account book recording expenditures for the relief of the Donner Party.

THE OLD SACRAMENTO TRAIL NORTH OF DONNER LAKE.